I'm Here for You

Written by: Amelia Riedler

Illustrated by: Dide Tengiz

I know that this moment, this phase, this unexpected chapter... it's more than overwhelming. I would give anything to take away your hurt—to make things lighter and easier, and to only give you life's good things.

You are so important to me.

I don't know what lies ahead—what challenges you'll navigate or moments you'll endure. But I do know I'm on this journey with you. And whatever the future may bring, I hope you remember...

If there are times you need a
listening ear when life gets loud,

Then I'm here to pour us some tea and hear all that you need to say. Because everything you're feeling is real.

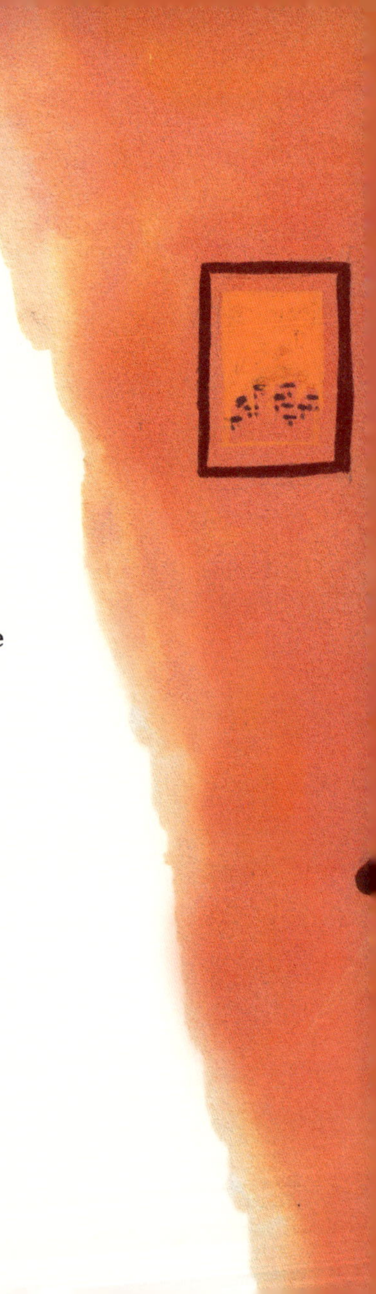

And if things are looking
dark and full of shadows,

I'm here to look up at the sky with you,
and I'll tell you how proud of you I am
for weathering this storm.

Or when everything is blurry and unsure,

I'm here to take your hand and remind you that you're strong and brave and honestly incredible.

I worry I don't know what to say, or when to say it. But I do know that helping you in any way I can is what I want most.

So if there are moments
when you feel small or alone,
or maybe not the hero
everyone expects you to be,

I'm here to sit quietly next to you.
It'll just be us, enjoying the simplicity
of time and each other's company.

Or if you feel less bright,
less shiny than you want to be,

I'm here to light a candle so we can reflect on the good things that bring us joy. And I will tell you that you are one of mine.

And when it's all too much to hold,

I'm here to shake things up with lightness and laughter—to distract us for a little while.

I know I can't change or magically fix this. But I do know that you will face all that comes with spirit and heart.

I know you will call on the courage
that's always been in you.

And I know you are enough,
exactly as you are right now.

More than anything, I know I'm on your side and by your side. I will try my hardest to support you in the ways that feel best to you. Whether that's a long hug or long phone call—or lots of space to be just where you are (however that might be).

Because through it all...

I'm here for you.

COMPENDIUM®
live inspired

This book was inspired by Sheila Kamuda, and written with love for Julie TeSelle.

Written by: Amelia Riedler
Illustrated by: Dide Tengiz
Edited by: Miriam Hathaway
Art Directed by: Jessica Phoenix

ISBN: 978-1-957891-55-2

1st printing. Printed in China with soy inks on FSC®-Mix certified paper.

Create meaningful moments with gifts that inspire.

CONNECT WITH US

live-inspired.com | sayhello@compendiuminc.com

@compendiumliveinspired
#compendiumliveinspired